CW00481579

OFFICIAL WORKBOOK for STOP OVERTHINKING:

A COMPANION WORKBOOK FOR NICK TRENTON'S INTERNATIONAL BESTSELLER

Table of Contents

CHAPTER 1: OVERTHINKING ISN'T ABOUT OVERTHINKING

When we're overthinking, our brains go into overdrive. Excessive thinking develops when our mental processes become out of control. A lifelong obsession with self- and life-analysis result in unwanted, uncontrollable, and self-defeating thoughts. Normally, our brains aid us in solving difficulties more effectively. An overactive mind engages in excessive mental activity, whether that activity is analysis or evaluation.

Typical overthinking tends to amplify itself or continue on indefinitely. If you have generalized anxiety or depression, overthinking may be a sign and manifestation of these problems as well. An example of overthinking is when we think about things that are disadvantageous to us. Overthinking diminishes the usefulness of our brain, which is a wonderful invention. Thought is a great gift, not a foe. It's not a bad thing to think.

In this first chapter of the workbook, let's get to know our brains a bit better. With the following thought-provoking questions/exercises, the goal is to reflect and gain awareness on our relationship with stress, the possible factors that can trigger our anxiety, and the consequences of overthinking.

Let's get started! Remember to answer the following questions honestly:

Describe a very stressful situation you encountered recently. How did you react to it?

_____

_____

_____

_____

_____

_____

Describe how you coped with that stressful situation. Was it helpful?

_____

_____

_____

_____

_____

_____

_____

_____

If ever you encounter the same stressful situation again, how would you approach it differently?

_____

_____

_____

_____

_____

_____

_____

_____

_____

_____

CAUSES OF MENTAL CLUTTER AND AGONY

There are two basic sources of anxiety. The first one is <u>ourselves</u>. Sadly, some of us are genetically predisposed to be more worried than the rest of the population. There are other factors at play as well. Overthinking might become a habit if it gives us the impression that we're making progress on the issue we're obsessing over. As a result of our constant overthinking, progress never happens, but we still feel like we're moving forward in some way. It can be difficult to break out of this vicious loop.

Another source of worry is our **environment**. For example: our immediate surroundings, such as our house and workplace, can contribute to our anxiety. The architecture of these rooms can have a significant impact on our levels of anxiety. Our anxiety levels will rise if they are cluttered, darkly lighted, or boisterous. As we connect with others, we gain a greater understanding of our social and cultural contexts. A stressful event, such as being the victim of racism or sexism, might increase our level of anxiety.

Reflect on how you experience anxiety. How does anxiety affect your day-to-day life?

_____

_____

_____

_____

_____

_____

_____

_____

_____

_____

_____

_____

_____

_____

_____

_____

_____

Let's take a look at the first source of anxiety: ourselves. Do you think that your anxiety is influenced by your family history, a medical condition, or a current lifestyle? Jot down your observations below. How frequently does this happen? What do you think you can do to change it?

_____

_____

_____

_____

_____

_____

_____

_____

_____

_____

_____

_____

_____

_____

_____

_____

_____

Let's proceed to the second source: environment. Do you think your anxiety is affected by external pressures such as life events (work pressures, traumatic events, etc.) or environmental factors (space, lighting, clutter, etc.)? Jot down your observations below. How frequently does this happen? What do you think you can do to change it?

_____

_____

_____

_____

_____

_____

_____

_____

_____

_____

_____

_____

_____

_____

_____

_____

_____

Think about three things that make you anxious and identify their possible sources:

Anxious Thought	Possible Source
("I am anxious about public speaking," or, "I am extremely worried about my health.")	*("I experienced being humiliated in public as a child."* *"My mom and dad have a history of cancer.")*

What are your current strategies to help yourself manage these triggers? Are they working?

_____

_____

_____

_____

_____

_____

_____

_____

_____

Complete the sentence: To prepare for future anxiety-inducing events, I will make the following changes . . .

_____

_____

_____

_____

_____

_____

_____

_____

_____

_____

THE SECRET INGREDIENT: OUR MENTAL MODELS

Our distinctive cognitive style, our mental frames, and the conduct that these inspire in us all play a significant role in determining whether we experience anxiety. The tale we tell about our life, the way we make sense of things, and our inner dialogue and sense of our own identity lie at the meeting point of nature and nurture. Stress and overwhelming events are determined by your interpretation and understanding of the situation.

When you encounter a stressful event, do you look at it as an opportunity or a threat?

_____

_____

_____

_____

_____

_____

_____

_____

_____

Are you satisfied with how you respond to stressful events? Why or why not?

_____

_____

_____

_____

_____

_____

_____

_____

_____

_____

Is there anything else you would like to change or improve on how you view a stressful event?

_____

_____

_____

_____

_____

_____

_____

_____

_____

What do you think is the cause for your current style of facing your problems?

_____

_____

_____

_____

_____

_____

_____

_____

_____

_____

CONSEQUENCES OF OVERTHINKING

Worry and overthinking aren't considered damaging because they're only thoughts, right? But that's not true. We have discovered how anxiety is a physical, mental, psychological, social, and even spiritual phenomenon. Everyone's predispositions and levels of resiliency are unique to each individual. We all have varying levels of exposure to environmental stressors. But the most important thing we can control is how we evaluate our experiences and go on.

Circle the effects you experience whenever you are overthinking:

Physical effects:

Racing heart	Headache	Nausea
Muscle tension	Aching muscles	Trembling
Sweating	Disturbed digestion	Immune system suppression
Memory issues	Insomnia	Fatigue
Dry mouth	Dizzy feelings	Others: _____

Mental effects:

Exhaustion	Fatigue	Feeling on edge
Inability to concentrate	Lack of motivation	Changes in libido
Nightmares	Depression	Sweating
Apathy	Lack of confidence	Harmful self-talk
Irritability	Changes in appetite	Others: _____

Social/environmental effects:

Damage to close relationships	Poor work performance	Impatience
Social avoidance	Stop making plans	Others: _____

When you experience these effects, what do you usually do to calm yourself down? Were your tactics effective in reducing your distress?

_____

_____

_____

_____

_____

_____

_____

_____

_____

Which physical/mental effects do you think are related to your beliefs, and which are easy to change via lifestyle?

_____

_____

_____

_____

_____

_____

_____

_____

_____

What lifestyle changes could you make?

_____

_____

_____

_____

_____

_____

_____

_____

What beliefs might those be?

_____

_____

_____

_____

_____

_____

_____

_____

_____

_____

_____

_____

If you have a friend who is also experiencing the same consequences as you, how do you think you would help them?

_____

_____

_____

_____

_____

_____

_____

_____

_____

_____

_____

_____

_____

_____

_____

_____

_____

_____

_____

_____

CHAPTER SUMMARY AND TAKEAWAYS

- What is overthinking, exactly? It's when you can't stop analyzing, evaluating, ruminating, or worrying about something and it starts to affect your mental health.
- People worry and think too much because of two main things: their genes and their environment. Some people are more likely to be anxious because their genes make them that way.
- In terms of environment, our immediate surroundings and how we interact with others can also impact our anxiety.
- Many harmful effects can come with overthinking. These include harms physically, mentally, and socially that can last for a long time.

CHAPTER 2: THE DE-STRESS FORMULA AND THEN SOME

In this second chapter of the workbook, we will explore self-awareness, stress management, and other techniques to de-stress.

Understanding why we overanalyze helps us relax. Overthinking causes and effects must be identified. Understanding the process improves decision-making. Don't know where to start? Let's start with awareness first.

Although ruminating can be a form of awareness, it is not the same as simply paying attention to our thoughts and feelings. Overthinkers need to learn how to tell the difference between being aware and being anxious. You can practice self-awareness by simply noticing and responding to bodily sensations (thinking and feeling) and by practicing mindfulness.

Do you observe any bodily sensations or reactions whenever you are anxious? (Ex. shaking hands, headaches, etc.)

_____

_____

_____

_____

_____

_____

_____

What kind of feelings do you have when you are anxious? (Ex. sad, irritable, panicky, etc.)

_____

_____

_____

_____

_____

_____

_____

_____

_____

_____

What kind of thoughts go through your head when you are anxious? (Ex. "I just want this to end," "This is making me crazy," etc.)

_____

_____

_____

_____

_____

_____

_____

_____

_____

How do you respond to these reactions when you are anxious? Are these responses effective?

_____

_____

_____

_____

_____

_____

_____

_____

_____

On a scale of 1-10, how aware do you think you are of your own thoughts and feelings when you are anxious?

_____

_____

_____

_____

_____

_____

_____

_____

_____

Do you think your current self-awareness level has helped you manage your anxiety better? Why or why not?

_____

_____

_____

_____

_____

_____

_____

_____

_____

THE 4 A's of STRESS MANAGEMENT

This technique was first proposed by the Mayo Clinic but is now used worldwide by therapists, coaches, doctors, and laypeople. Having a simple, structured approach to anxiety can help in times of stress and overthinking. All you need to do is **avoid**, **alter**, **accept**, and **adapt**. It can be comforting to know there are four primary ways to handle stress.

Let's explore the first way: **avoid**.

Many irritations can be avoided by simply walking away. We can't control everything, but we can avoid stressful situations and people. If we're honest, we may realize that much of our stress is voluntary—and we don't have to accept it. You're not avoiding obligations or problems by avoiding stress. You're learning to reject harmful, unnecessary stress. We can always say no to people and situations that demand too much.

Mental energy, attention, and time are resources.

In the original book, one example is to consider someone who dislikes Saturday-morning grocery shopping. Knowing that this stresses them out, they can shop on a Tuesday evening instead when it's quietest. Avoiding a busy supermarket saves them stress.

Now, let's see how you can manage your stress by just simply **avoiding** it.

Think of a situation that really stresses you out. What do you think you can realistically do to avoid it? Think outside the box, or think about drawing boundaries with people or situations.

_____

_____

_____

_____

_____

_____

_____

_____

Do you think avoidance is an effective way to manage your stress? Why or why not?

_____

_____

_____

_____

_____

_____

_____

_____

_____

Second, if you can't avoid it, you might need to find ways to change the situation—i.e., **alter** it.

We can't avoid stress, but we can change its course. We have the power to change the situation. Share your needs and ask for what you want with "I" statements. To relax on Saturday, listen to an audiobook on your phone. Mix PTA meetings with other errands to save time, effort, and gas. Reducing unavoidable situations can help. If you can't avoid the party, say, "I have to leave in an hour—early start tomorrow!"

Think about the stressful situation you thought of in the previous exercise. If it cannot be avoided, what can you do to change or reduce it to a less stressful situation? How can you shape this situation to meet your needs?

_____

_____

_____

_____

_____

_____

_____

_____

Do you think altering the situation is an effective way to manage your stress? Why or why not?

_____

_____

_____

_____

_____

_____

_____

_____

If changing the situation is not a good option for you, then we might need to go with the third way: **accept.**

How do you accept a bad situation? If you hate it, hate it. Acceptance is acknowledging that it's okay to feel how you feel. Own your feelings. Acceptance may involve forgiving if you've been wronged. You forgive yourself, not the other person. When you forgive, you free yourself from resentment and blame. Acceptance may also involve framing events differently. We can't change events, but we can change how we talk about them. Instead of, "I failed my course and wasted money, I'm an idiot," you could say, "I messed up this time by not working harder. This doesn't define me. Mistakes can be overcome. Next time, I'll do better."

Acceptance doesn't mean we like what happened or shouldn't change it. We accept

what we can't change so we can focus on what
we can.

**Recall the stressful situation you thought
of in the previous exercises. If it cannot be
avoided or changed, what can you do to
accept it instead?**

_____

_____

_____

_____

_____

_____

_____

_____

_____

Should you accept it? Why or why not?

_____

_____

_____

_____

_____

_____

_____

_____

What are the negative consequences of accepting it?

_____

_____

_____

_____

_____

_____

_____

_____

_____

Will this be better for you overall, or worse?

_____

_____

_____

_____

_____

_____

_____

_____

_____

_____

_____

Is it truly adapting, or is it just acceptance? Or is it something you should actually avoid or alter instead? Why?

_____

_____

_____

_____

_____

_____

_____

_____

_____

_____

_____

_____

_____

_____

_____

_____

_____

_____

_____

_____

Let's practice reframing the way you think or talk about what stresses you out, by turning unhelpful thoughts into useful/positive ones. Fill out the table below:

(NOTE: For the last rows, use thoughts from the stressful event you you thought of in the previous exercises.)

UNHELPFUL THOUGHTS *Instead of . . .*	REFRAMED THOUGHTS *Try to say . . .*
Example: *I completely failed my course and wasted my money. I'm such an idiot for not working harder.*	Example: *I made a mistake and I'm not happy about it. But this one event doesn't define me. I can learn from mistakes and move on. I will do better next time.*

UNHELPFUL THOUGHTS	REFRAMED THOUGHTS
Instead of . . .	*Try to say . . .*
I don't know what's wrong with me. I can't seem to do anything right. I always fail.	
I had an argument with my partner. I feel so stupid.	

Do you think accepting the situation is an effective way to manage your stress? Why or why not?

_____

_____

_____

_____

_____

_____

_____

_____

_____

_____

_____

_____

The last way is to: **adapt.** Stress helps us adapt long term. Adapting involves changing our worldview, goals, perception, and expectations. Imagine a stressed-out perfectionist who never meets expectations. Instead of being Superman, lower your expectations. Adapting to stress means coping. Avoid negative thoughts and be optimistic. Stress adaptation builds resilience. Our worldviews empower. Someone may keep a daily "gratitude list," and another person may meditate on a personal "code" or daily mantra to remind them they're strong. We can handle stress if we have powerful attitudes, ideas, philosophies, and inspiration.

In general, do you view stressful situations as a crisis or a challenge? Are you content with this perspective, or is there anything you would like to change about it?

_____

_____

_____

_____

_____

_____

_____

_____

_____

_____

_____

_____

_____

Which of your standards or expectations can you adjust to respond to a stressful situation? Do you think that you need to adapt? Or do you just need to accept? Is it something you should actually avoid or alter instead?

_____

_____

_____

_____

_____

_____

_____

_____

_____

_____

_____

_____

_____

_____

_____

_____

_____

_____

_____

Let's create a list of five things you are thankful for.

(NOTE: Feel free to look back on this during a stressful situation to calm your mind.)

1._____
2._____
3._____
4._____
5._____

Now, let's create a MANTRA. Construct a positive affirmation that you can repeat daily to remind yourself that you are strong, and write it inside the box. (Ex. I can do this! I am resilient and brave!)

Out of the four A's of stress management (avoid, alter, accept, and adapt), which do you think are the most helpful to you? Which do you think are the least helpful? Identify how to use the four A's of stress management in three areas down below for immediate action.

_____

_____

_____

_____

_____

_____

_____

_____

_____

_____

_____

_____

_____

_____

_____

_____

_____

STRESS DIARIES AND JOURNALS

Writing down your stress can help you better understand it. Overthinking can make it seem like you have a million things to do at once, making it difficult to pinpoint the source of your anxiety. Positive affect journaling (PAJ) has been linked to better emotional self-regulation, improved wellbeing, and fewer depression and anxiety symptoms.

In this section, let's try to do a little PAJ. Below are a few prompts for you to answer. Take your time and try to focus on positive emotions while answering them:

Even though I've had a bad day, I can't help but smile when . . .

Is there anything I require to feel safe, secure, and heard when things get tough? Do I have it in me to do that?

_____

_____

_____

_____

_____

_____

_____

_____

_____

_____

_____

_____

_____

_____

_____

_____

_____

_____

_____

_____

_____

Whenever I encounter a stressful situation, I think that it's teaching me to . . .

_____

_____

_____

_____

_____

_____

_____

_____

_____

_____

_____

_____

_____

_____

_____

_____

_____

_____

_____

_____

What qualities do I love about myself? Why?

What are things that give me a sense of well-being and purpose? How can I add more of them to my life?

_____

_____

_____

_____

_____

_____

_____

_____

_____

_____

_____

_____

_____

_____

_____

_____

_____

_____

_____

_____

Who has inspired me to be the person I want to be? What characteristics do I admire in them?

_____

_____

Visualize a happy self. Draw how you would look if you were stress-free.

Reflect. How did you feel about the journaling activity? Was it helpful in regulating your emotions and stress levels? Did thinking about happy or positive thoughts change your stress levels?

_____

_____

_____

_____

_____

_____

_____

_____

_____

_____

_____

_____

_____

_____

_____

_____

_____

_____

_____

_____

Journaling isn't used only this way. A **stress diary** can help you pinpoint triggers and reactions. You can then start managing your stress. A stress diary is a written record of your stress and related information that you can analyze and use to manage stress. This diary can help us determine our ideal stress level. An entry in a stress diary can go like this:

4 February, 9:15

Received a worrying message about Dad needing surgery on his shoulder. Feeling around 4/10, kind of apprehensive and a little tired. Weird knot feeling in my stomach. Trouble staying focused on work: only working at about 1/10 effectiveness. I think I feel this way because I'm worried about something bad happening to him. I'm avoiding replying to the message, but I think this is making my anxiety worse.

Now, it's your turn. Following the example above, write your entries in the provided

boxes below. They don't have to be done every day. Only log entries when you feel a mood shift or when you're noticeably stressed. Once you've completed the five entries, you can decide whether you want to keep your own stress diary or not:

For each entry, record the time, date, and how you feel. You can use a rating scale (1 for not stressed, 10 for super stressed), feeling words, or physical symptoms (like sweaty palms). Scale your effectiveness and productivity. Note any recent stressful events and possible causes of your current state. Note how you responded and the outcome. (Use the diary entry boxes on the next pages.)

Diary Entry #1

Diary Entry #2

Diary Entry #3

Diary Entry #4

Diary Entry #5

Once you've completed the five entries, let's sit down and analyze to find any patterns. Answer the questions below:

What are the most frequent causes of stress? What usually comes before a sudden rise in stress or drop in mood?

_____
_____
_____
_____
_____
_____
_____

How do these events typically affect your productivity and mood?

_____
_____
_____
_____
_____
_____
_____

_____

_____

How do you normally respond emotionally and behaviorally to these events, and is your approach working?

_____

_____

_____

_____

_____

_____

_____

_____

Can you identify a level of stress that was comfortable and beneficial for your productivity?

_____

_____

_____

_____

_____

_____

_____

_____

_____
_____

Reflect. How did you feel about the stress diary activity? What pattern were you able to uncover? Was the diary helpful in reducing and understanding your stress? Did getting things out of your brain and onto paper allow you to let go a little bit?

_____
_____
_____
_____
_____
_____
_____
_____
_____
_____
_____
_____
_____
_____
_____
_____
_____

THE 5-4-3-2-1 GROUNDING TECHNIQUE

Regularly using stress journals and the 4 A's technique can be very effective, but sometimes you need instant stress relief. The 5-4-3-2-1 grounding technique helps panic attack sufferers stop their anxiety spiral before it gets out of control. You don't need to have a panic disorder to do this, though.

Overthinking is controlled in the same way as complex fears and phobias. Overthinking, ruminating, and stressing take us out of the moment. We mull over the past or future. We wonder "what if" and obsess over memories, ideas, probabilities, wishes, and fears.

If we focus on the present, we can stop overthinking. The five senses help us do this. The brain can take you everywhere, but the body and its senses are always present.

The technique is simple:

1. Find **five** things you can see
2. Find **four** things you can touch
3. Find **three** things you can hear
4. Find **two** things you can smell
5. Find **one** thing you can taste

This exercise is a distraction.

When your senses are active, your brain is distracted from endless rumination and overthinking. Try it! When you catch yourself stressing, you can do this technique on your own or turn to this part of the workbook. See the table on the next page.

5	Things you can see	**1.** **2.** **3.** **4.** **5.**
4	Things you can touch	**1.** **2.** **3.** **4.**
3	Things you can hear	**1.** **2.** **3.**
2	Things you can smell	**1.** **2.**
1	Thing you can taste	**1.**

How did you feel when you were able to focus on other things besides your stressful thoughts? Did you notice a difference?

_____

_____

_____

_____

_____

_____

_____

_____

Do you think this technique is helpful in putting you back in the present? Would you do it regularly? Why or why not?

_____

_____

_____

_____

_____

_____

_____

Another way is to try **literal grounding**. Gaétan Chevalier found that "earthing" or grounding the body affected mood. Chevalier asked study participants to spend an hour on the ground. He then tested them and found a statistically significant boost in self-reported moods and wellbeing in those who were in contact with the earth. This finding is encouraging, but it's unlikely to be enough to treat a serious anxiety disorder.

Let's try literal grounding. Go outside and try to be in contact with the earth for at least fifteen minutes. How did you feel? Were there any changes in your mood?

_____

_____

_____

_____

_____

_____

_____

_____

_____

_____

Do you think this technique is helpful in putting you back in the present? Would you do it regularly? Why or why not?

_____

_____

_____

_____

_____

_____

_____

_____

_____

_____

Which grounding technique was the most helpful to you? Why?

_____

_____

_____

_____

_____

_____

_____

_____

_____

NARRATIVE THERAPY AND EXTERNALIZATION

Narrative therapy explores how our lives are often viewed as stories, or narratives. People make meaning by telling stories about themselves and their lives. Narrative therapy rewrites these stories to find healing and a happy ending.

Part of overcoming anxiety is examining our mental models and deciding how to live. When we tell our own stories, we take charge, reframe, and make new meanings. This idea underpins a popular technique called "externalization" in narrative therapy.

We externalize the problem. We don't judge or blame ourselves for having problems. We can make meaningful changes in how we talk about ourselves and our lives. Realize that you are in control and the author of your own experience. Other people are not to blame for our perception, and they cannot save or teach us; we are the experts of our own experience.

Think of a problem that has been bothering you lately. What would you like to call it? How do you visualize it? Feel free to be creative and draw it in the box below:

Give your problem a name:

_____

As you proceed with the exercises, don't forget to write the name of your problem on the blank provided in each question.

Describe _____ **(the name of your problem). How does it affect your daily life and** **relationships?**

_____

_____

_____

_____

_____

_____

_____

Let's evaluate _____ **(the name of your problem). Are you accepting what it is doing? Are its effects favorable to you or not?**

_____

_____

_____

_____

_____

_____

_____

Why do you think you are giving _____ (the name of your problem) so much value?

_____

_____

_____

_____

_____

_____

_____

_____

_____

What do you think your position would be without _____ (the name of your problem)?

_____

_____

_____

_____

_____

_____

_____

_____

What steps would you take to be distant from _____ (the name of your problem)?

_____

_____

_____

_____

_____

_____

_____

_____

_____

Write the name of the problem on a separate piece of paper. Next, throw, crumple, or burn the paper. (NOTE: You can pick one or do everything.)

Which of the options did you do? How did it feel afterward?

_____

_____

_____

_____

_____

_____

Reflect. Did externalizing the problem help you see your problem objectively? Why or why not?

_____

_____

_____

_____

_____

_____

_____

_____

_____

_____

_____

_____

_____

_____

_____

_____

_____

_____

_____

_____

_____

Another technique that narrative therapy uses is deconstruction. When you overthink, you feel overwhelmed: a million thoughts are racing through your head at once, and you don't know where to begin. Stories are sequential, which is fantastic. Stories can help us analyze a big, terrifying situation if we're lost in rumination.

A story helps you organize, slow down, and focus your attention. Not everything can be viewed simultaneously. Trying to do too much often makes you feel helpless and small. As in any good novel, you don't have to solve everything at once.

Let's try to construct a story about what has been bothering you lately. Using the box below, imagine you're an author writing a story based on your stressful event:

Title of your story

Based on the story you wrote above, describe the problem that the protagonist/main character is experiencing.

_____

_____

_____

_____

_____

_____

_____

_____

What do you think caused the main character's problem? How could they have prevented it?

_____

_____

_____

_____

_____

_____

_____

_____

How did the main character overcome the challenges that came their way? Are you satisfied with how they handled it? If not, what would you like to change about it?

_____

_____

_____

_____

_____

_____

What do you think is the moral lesson of the story you wrote?

_____

_____

_____

_____

_____

_____

_____

_____

_____

_____

_____

_____

If you were to revise the story, which parts would you change? Which would you leave untouched?

_____

_____

_____

_____

_____

_____

_____

_____

_____

_____

_____

_____

_____

_____

_____

_____

_____

_____

_____

_____

_____

_____

_____

Reflect. Did writing a story help you deconstruct your problem properly? Why or why not?

_____

_____

_____

_____

_____

_____

_____

_____

_____

_____

_____

_____

_____

_____

_____

_____

_____

_____

_____

_____

_____

_____

CHAPTER SUMMARY AND TAKEAWAYS

- There are simple yet effective ways to soothe an anxious, overthinking mind.
- Remember the 4 A's of stress management: avoid, alter, accept, and adapt. Avoiding mean staying clear of things you can't control. Some things aren't worth the trouble and should be eradicated. If we can't avoid the stressor, we must change our environment and accept the environment we can't change. If we can't change the situation, we must adapt and learn how to cope with the stressor to minimize its damage.
- Journaling is another method to quiet your mind. Overthinking causes us to have several thoughts at once, which is overpowering. When we write things down, we can examine if they're justified. To cultivate the habit, carry a pocket journal and write as needed.
- Another strategy is the 5-4-3-2-1 grounding technique. It uses all five senses to stop panic episodes.

Whenever you experience terror, look for five things you can see, four you can touch, three you can smell, two you can hear, and one you can taste. Sensory stimulation prevents overthinking.

- Deconstruction and externalization, some techniques from narrative therapy, are also other ways to help us create distance from our stressor, zoom out, and see the big picture.

CHAPTER 3: MANAGE YOUR TIME AND INPUTS

In the original book, we met Susie. Susie is a busy person. She looks at her schedule and panics about fitting everything in. Her coworker, seeing her agitated and overthinking, suggests lunchtime meditation because it reduces stress. Five minutes into meditation, Susie realizes she has even less time and can't focus because of her 2:30 appointment.

If bad time management causes our tension, traditional relaxing practices won't assist us. Susie would benefit from a time machine or a better schedule. Meditation, stretching, etc. can help us deal with stress, but we can reduce it by better organizing our time. This chapter of the workbook explains sensible and proven control approaches. But before we dive into that, let's take a look at how you manage your time.

When you have lots of things to do, how do you usually manage your time?

_____

_____

_____

_____

_____

_____

_____

How is the system working out for you? Does it contribute to your stress in some way? Is it efficient and effective?

_____

_____

_____

_____

_____

_____

_____

_____

_____

_____

_____

Do you think that your current time management strategy is effective? Is there anything you want to change about it?

_____

_____

_____

_____

_____

_____

_____

_____

_____

_____

_____

_____

_____

_____

_____

_____

_____

_____

_____

STRESS MANAGEMENT 101

Time management helps many people handle stress. Time management skills may aid you more than relaxing approaches can if you're anxious about deadlines, rushed, or overwhelmed.

Time management goes beyond multitasking. It helps you organize your life so you can focus on what's important. Not cramming as much work as possible into a day, but ensuring your life's proportions and priorities reflect your principles.

Make a list of your values and priorities in life. What are the three most important things in your life?

1._____

2._____

3._____

How do you usually spend your week? Fill out the table on the next page:

M	T	W	Th	F	S	S

Time (AM)
00:00
01:00
02:00
03:00
04:00
05:00
06:00
07:00
08:00
09:00
10:00
11:00

Time (PM)	M	T	W	Th	F	S	S
12:00							
01:00							
02:00							
03:00							
04:00							
05:00							
06:00							
07:00							
08:00							
09:00							
10:00							
11:00							

Using the table you filled out, let's analyze the data. Where do you spend the most time? How about the least amount of time?

_____

_____

_____

_____

_____

_____

_____

_____

_____

_____

Do you think your time usage aligns with the priorities you listed above?

_____

_____

_____

_____

_____

_____

_____

_____

_____

_____

Is there anything you'd like to change in your schedule to align it better with your priorities? If yes, what adjustments would you make?

_____

_____

_____

_____

_____

_____

_____

_____

_____

Circle the time management habit you're already practicing:

Creating to-do lists	Calendar scheduling	Habit or goal tracking
Breaking tasks into smaller ones	Prioritizing tasks based on urgency	Pomodoro technique
Thinking of the process before the outcome	Saying no	Setting deadlines

Which of the habits you circled is the most effective?

_____

_____

_____

_____

_____

_____

_____

_____

_____

_____

Which of the habits you did not circle is something you'd most likely try?

_____

_____

_____

_____

_____

_____

_____

_____

Is there any time management habit that you're doing or familiar with that is not in the list? If yes, write it down below and describe how it helped/can help you.

_____

_____

_____

_____

_____

_____

_____

_____

_____

_____

_____

_____

There is also a variety of time management styles or personas, not just strategies. How well (or poorly) you manage your own time may have a lot to do with the distinct differences between you and everyone else. In the original book, we explored these personas. As a recap, here's a table:

Time Management Persona	Description	Solution
Time Martyr	A person who accepts everyone's requests and takes on too much responsibility, and then pays the price.	Strict scheduling. Limiting tasks per day.
Procrastinator	Acts too late. Anxiety worsens procrastination.	Break things down into small tasks. Reward yourself per mini-milestone.
Distractor	Starts well but then becomes distracted and finds it hard to focus.	Set firmer boundaries. Consider environment you're working in.

Time Management Persona	Description	Solution
Underestimator	Underestimates the amount of time it will take to complete a task, which can result in missed deadlines.	Tackle projects step by step. Give time to appraise the process realistically.
Firefighter	Always on the go, putting out "fires" everywhere and juggling a zillion things at once, often at the height of a crisis.	Delegation. Prioritization.
Perfectionist	Never accomplishes anything because nothing ever satisfies their vision of perfection.	Boundary setting. Realistic planning. Delegating.

Which time management persona resonates with you the most? Why?

_____

_____

_____

_____

_____

_____

_____

_____

_____

_____

_____

_____

_____

_____

_____

_____

_____

_____

_____

_____

_____

What solutions are you currently doing to manage your time? Does it align with the solutions for the time management persona you've identified with?

_____

_____

_____

_____

_____

_____

_____

_____

Which of the other listed solutions would you be willing to give a try? Do you think it will be helpful to you? Which will you commit to trying for the next two weeks?

_____

_____

_____

_____

_____

_____

_____

_____

HOW TO MANAGE YOUR TIME, ENERGY, AND INPUTS

If you're struggling to manage your time effectively, here are a few ideas to consider. The following might work for you depending on your personal time management style and lifestyle. Let's explore them one by one.

Allen's Input Processing Technique

This method helps procrastinators, firemen, and distractors navigate our information-saturated world. With this technique, data is dubbed "inputs," or any environmental stimulus: meetings, emails, phone calls, social media, TV, etc. How do you respond to these hooks? Allen's technique says that unless you plan ahead, you'll respond poorly.

To help you visualize it, here's a sample chart:

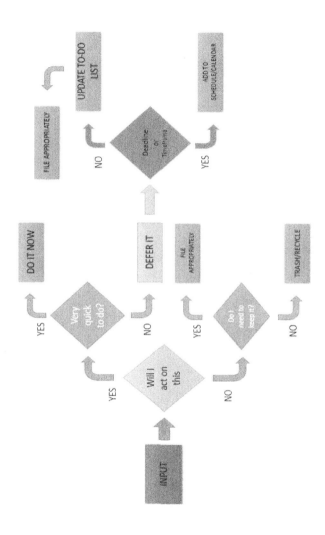

INPUT

Will I act on this

YES → Very quick to do?
- YES → DO IT NOW
- NO → DEFER IT

NO → Do I need to keep it?
- YES → FILE APPROPRIATELY
- NO → TRASH/RECYCLE

Deadline or Timeframe
- NO → FILE APPROPRIATELY → UPDATE TO-DO LIST
- YES → ADD TO SCHEDULE/CALENDAR

With a strategy, you don't have to waste time and energy examining each new input; you can make a quick decision and move on to what's important. Identify your major inputs by monitoring your day-to-day existence. What matters is that they catch your eye. What's your response? Will you act?

Using the chart above, replace input with something that you have been struggling with or stresses you out. Where did your response lead you?

_____

_____

_____

_____

_____

Using the chart, determine what you have observed about your decision-making. Were you able to make decisions swiftly or did you take your time?

_____

_____

_____

_____

Upon doing this activity, what have you realized about your own workflow? Did this chart change something about how you manage your time?

_____

_____

_____

_____

_____

Do you think this technique is helpful in managing your stress? Why or why not?

_____

_____

_____

_____

_____

_____

_____

_____

_____

_____

Eisenhower's Method

Good time management boils down to identifying your priorities and allowing them to influence your activities and goal-setting. This strategy is wonderful for firefighters, perfectionists, and time martyrs because it challenges us to tackle a task efficiently when we may not have enough time or resources.

The need to juggle an excessive number of commitments with an inadequate amount of time or resources is the basis of much unnecessary overthinking. This leads to stress, which in turn feeds overthinking. Even if we are unable to prevent such time pressure, we are surely able to adjust it or adapt ourselves to it. The reality for many of us is that we have an excessive amount of work to complete in a limited amount of time. The approach of Urgent/Important, developed by former president of the United States Dwight D. Eisenhower, can be of assistance and allow you to cut through what is actually important and what merely serves as a distraction.

Confused? Let's understand the labels better:

Important tasks help us reach our aim.
Urgent jobs need rapid attention because of a penalty for not doing so.

As you can see, the box is divided into four quadrants to help you assess your tasks:

- important and urgent
- important but not urgent
- not important but urgent
- not important and not urgent.

Basically, the Eisenhower Method is a task management tool that organizes and prioritizes tasks. Using the tool, you'll divide your tasks into four boxes: what you will do, what you will decide to do later, what you will delegate, and what you will delete/eliminate.

Let's classify your tasks. List what you consider <u>important and urgent</u>.

_____

_____

_____

_____

_____

_____

For the tasks you consider <u>important and urgent</u>, do you do them immediately? If not, what is preventing you from doing this? What adjustments will you make so you can do these tasks immediately?

_____

_____

_____

_____

_____

List tasks that are <u>important but not urgent.</u>

_____

_____

_____

_____

_____

_____

_____

_____

For the tasks you consider <u>important but not urgent</u>, do you decide or schedule when to do them? If not, what is preventing you from doing this? What adjustments will you make so you can schedule properly?

_____

_____

_____

_____

_____

_____

_____

_____

_____

List tasks that are not **important but urgent**.

_____

_____

_____

_____

_____

For the tasks you consider not **important but urgent**, do you delegate them? If not, what is preventing you from doing this? What adjustments will you make so you can delegate properly?

_____

_____

_____

_____

_____

_____

List tasks that are not **important and not urgent**.

_____

_____

_____

_____

For the tasks you consider <u>not important and not urgent</u>, do you eliminate them? If not, what is preventing you from doing this? What adjustments will you make so you can delete these tasks off your list?

_____

_____

_____

_____

_____

_____

Do you think the Eisenhower Method can be effective in helping you prioritize your tasks and manage your stress? Why or why not?

_____

_____

_____

_____

_____

_____

_____

_____

_____

SMART Goals

SMART goals are specific, measurable, achievable, relevant, and timely. In *The Power of SMART Goals: Using Goals to Improve Student Learning*, Jan O'Neill discusses clear, achievable goals and measured success. Goal-setting prevents overthinking. Uncertainty, haziness, and scattered options cause stress and ruminating. We feel in control when we shape the unknown.

Goals reduce noise and distraction to improve focus. Values don't ensure goal-setting success. Set realistic goals. SMART goals help you succeed. Before we practice setting SMART goals, let's take a look at your current goal system:

Do you set goals regularly? If yes, how do you set them? If not, why?

_____

_____

_____

_____

_____

Are you consistent in achieving your goals? If yes, what contributes to this success? If not, what do you think is lacking in your process?

_____

_____

_____

_____

_____

_____

Do you experience any difficulty whenever you set goals? How do you plan to address them?

_____

_____

_____

_____

_____

_____

_____

_____

_____

_____

_____

_____

Let's set goals using the SMART method. Think of a current goal you are pursuing and then fill out the table below:

Specific (What do you want to accomplish?)	*(Ex. I want to change my career path.)*
Measurable (How will you measure your progress?)	*(Ex. I need to get at least five job interviews in the industry I'm transitioning to.)*
Attainable (How can the goal be accomplished?)	*(Ex. I need to upskill and prepare a portfolio, update my CV, and then send my resume to potential employers.)*
Relevant (Is the goal aligned with my objectives?)	*(Ex. This goal will help me grow professionally.)*
Time-bound (How long will it take for me to accomplish my goals?)	*(Ex. I want to be able to transition to a new industry in three to six months.)*

Do you think the SMART method can be effective in helping you accomplish your goals and manage your stress? Why or why not?

_____

_____

_____

_____

_____

_____

_____

_____

_____

_____

_____

_____

_____

_____

_____

_____

_____

_____

_____

_____

Kanban Method

The more information you can get out of your head (by being organized and efficient), the less you'll worry and overthink. Many of Kanban's ideas can boost your own productivity. This strategy improves workflow. The Japanese Kanban system was developed to maximize factory productivity. Kanban can help improve personal systems and procedures. It can't help you define goals or create systems, but it can streamline existing ones. A common Kanban board looks like this, usually with sticky notes:

TO DO	DOING	DONE

In the original book, The Kanban Method is explained to follow four foundational principles:

1. Start with what you're already doing

2. Make constant, incremental changes for the better

3. Respect current rules and limitations (at least initially)

4. Think about encouraging leadership wherever possible

As individuals, we're more interested in the second concept of ongoing development. Small, cumulative increments are more effective than massive (intimidating) quantum leaps.

Let's try to do the Kanban Method in this workbook.

Grab a pencil and eraser, then list at least three tasks in the "To Do" column.

TO DO	DOING	DONE

Once you've listed the tasks, pick one that you will do first. Erase it and write it in the "Doing" column.

When you're done with that task, erase it again and write it in the "Done" column. Simple, right? Try doing the same for the other two tasks.

Using the Kanban Method, what did you observe about your workflow? How did the attention, time, and energy flow from task to task? Were you able to switch tasks smoothly? Or did you face distractions in between?

_____

_____

_____

_____

_____

_____

_____

What did you like most about your workflow? What did you like the least?

_____

_____

_____

_____

_____

_____

_____

_____

_____

Is there something you would change in your process to maximize your productivity and improve your workflow?

_____

_____

_____

_____

_____

_____

Time Blocking

Most people spend their days working. It's easy to waste time on meetings, emails, and "busy work" that fosters overthinking. Firefighters, procrastinators, and time martyrs who wish to reduce stress could use time blocking. It can help you shift out of a reactive, distracted state and prevent chaotic days.

Instead of multitasking or quickly switching between tasks, time blocking allows you to focus on one task at a time. By planning ahead, you waste no time or willpower making decisions and can start with your priorities.

You want "deep work" and interest in what you're doing, not shallow multitasking. This is effective (you get more done in a set time) and less stressful, and you may get more out of work with less mental or emotional effort.

To get started with time blocking, we will be using this table on the next page:

Time (AM)	Activity
00:00	
01:00	
02:00	
03:00	
04:00	
05:00	
06:00	
07:00	
08:00	
09:00	
10:00	
11:00	

Time (PM)	Activity
00:00	
01:00	
02:00	
03:00	
04:00	
05:00	
06:00	
07:00	
08:00	
09:00	
10:00	
11:00	

For this simple activity, pick any day from Monday to Sunday. What do you hope to achieve on that day? List three things that you are willing to prioritize.

_____

_____

_____

_____

_____

_____

_____

Do you have any morning or evening routines that you want to establish? If yes, what are those? What specific time in the morning or evening do you want to do them? (Fill out the table above after answering this question.)

_____

_____

_____

_____

_____

_____

_____

Using the table above, set a time for the three priority tasks you mentioned. Do you think you will be able to commit to your own schedule?

_____

_____

_____

_____

_____

_____

_____

Based on your current schedule, do you think you have room for tasks you consider shallow and less important? If yes, how much time will you allot for them? (Fill out the table above after answering this question.)

_____

_____

_____

_____

_____

_____

_____

_____

Take a look at the schedule you made above. Are you satisfied with your schedule? Do you think this schedule helps you focus more on what to accomplish?

_____

_____

_____

_____

_____

_____

_____

Do you think time blocking is an effective way to manage someone's stress? Why or why not?

_____

_____

_____

_____

_____

_____

_____

_____

CHAPTER SUMMARY AND TAKEAWAYS

- Poor time management contributes to anxiety. We prioritize things that make us unhappy and neglect things we like. We rarely relax enough, so we must do it purposely to reduce our worry. Making regular to-do lists, prioritizing work, and dividing goals into smaller pieces are some strategies.

- There are alternative time-management solutions. Allen's input processing technique is one. External stimuli are inputs. Analyze and note how you respond to calls, emails, etc. Then, plan the best strategy to respond based on your existing responses to prioritize certain stimuli. Another technique is the Eisenhower Method. This tool helps you prioritize tasks and decide which jobs to do first and which to assign or delete.

- SMART goals are also helpful. Detailed goals help you know what to do. Set criteria for achieving this aim. Make sure the aim is reasonable; don't be unrealistic. Assess how this objective fits your values and what it will accomplish for you. Set a fair deadline for finishing this goal.

- Other techniques are the Kanban Method and time blocking. The Japanese Kanban began as a strategy to organize industries for optimal efficiency. Personal Kanban is helpful for enhancing ongoing systems and processes. Time blocking can restrain perfectionist tendencies and create a more realistic timeline.

CHAPTER 4: HOW TO FIND INSTANT ZEN

Planning and organizing your time according to your beliefs and goals reduces stress and overthinking. But despite the best-laid strategies, sometimes you still overthink. In place of nervous over-rumination, another thing you can do is breathing and thinking about purposeful activities you'd like to do. Learning to relax is important. Relaxing lowers your heart rate, breathing, and blood pressure, improves digestion and blood sugar, moderates stress chemicals in the body, reduces weariness and muscle ache, and boosts focus, sleep, and confidence. This reduces anxiety and ruminating.

In this chapter of the workbook, we'll develop a habit of relaxing through some relaxation techniques: autogenic training, guided imagery and visualization, progressive relaxation muscle, and worry postponement. Don't worry! This workbook will be with you throughout the process. You'll be practicing these techniques with the steps provided. After every exercise, there will be questions that you will need to answer honestly. It's a good way to see if you found the technique effective and helpful.

Are you ready to do the techniques? But before that, let's first assess your idea of relaxation:

What do you do to relax and clear your mind? Make a list of your relaxing activities below.

_____

_____

_____

_____

_____

_____

_____

_____

_____

_____

_____

_____

How often do you do these relaxing activities? Do you find time to do them?

_____

_____

_____

_____

_____

_____

_____

_____

_____

_____

Whenever you do a relaxing activity, what changes do you notice in your body and mood?

_____

_____

_____

_____

_____

_____

_____

_____

_____

_____

Do you think they are effective? Why or why not?

_____

_____

_____

_____

_____

_____

_____

_____

_____

What do you think would work that you haven't tried?

_____

_____

_____

_____

_____

_____

_____

_____

_____

AUTOGENIC TRAINING

Johannes Schultz, a 1920s hypnotist and relaxation enthusiast, created autogenic relaxation. Autogenic training produces a calm body and mind on command. Autogenic training reduces nurses' perceived stress, according to *Asian Nursing Research*. Autogenic training lowered stress during Spain's Covid-19 epidemic in 2021, according to Rivera and colleagues.

Six techniques encompass body and mind, and these sessions usually last around twenty minutes. The "trainee" may start in a comfortable position while the trainer describes body feelings. The trainer may repeat, "I am completely calm," five or six times, then, "My right arm is heavy," "I am completely calm," "My left arm is heavy," etc. After the treatment, statements like, "My arm has firmed up," and, "I'm alert," are used to awaken from the relaxation.

As a recap, the six techniques or "lessons" use cues that promote awareness of the following:

- Heaviness
- Warmth
- Awareness of heartbeat
- Awareness of breath
- Awareness of abdominal sensations
- Focus on coolness of the forehead

At the end of each session, the learner has learned to relax and better control their awareness of stimuli. By using these strategies, you gain empowerment and control over your inner world.

Are you ready? Let's try to run a session. Follow these steps carefully:

1. Find a comfortable position—sitting or lying down—take some slow, deep breaths, and begin by slowly repeating to yourself six times, "I am completely calm." If you are doing the second "lesson," for example, you can focus on warmth. Put your

awareness onto sensations of warmth in your body.

2. Then repeat, also six times, "My left arm is warm," followed by six repetitions of, "I am completely calm." Say this slowly and really engage with the sensations, slowing your breath and focusing only on your body.

3. Follow up with your other arm, both legs, chest, and abdomen, alternating with, "I am completely calm."

4. Reverse the process by saying, "Arms, firm up," "I am alert," and so on, and finally, "Eyes open," as you end the session. It should take fifteen to twenty minutes total.

NOTE: Each time you try this, focus on a different sensation, such as heaviness, warmth, heartbeat, etc. You can then combine the sessions.

Ex:

"My arms are heavy."
"My legs are warm."
"My heartbeat is calm and regular."
"My breath is calm and regular."
"My abdomen is relaxed."
"My forehead is pleasantly cool."

It's vital to take your time and feel the sensations. Don't rush; focus on calming yourself. "I'm calm" calms your body.

After doing your autogenic training, take the time to answer the questions below:

How did you feel about the autogenic training? What did you like and dislike about it?

_____

_____

_____

_____

_____

_____

_____

Was it effective? Were you able to relax throughout the activity?

_____

_____

_____

_____

_____

_____

_____

_____

_____

_____

What did you think about the process? Did you find it easy or difficult to focus on one sensation to another?

_____

_____

_____

_____

_____

_____

_____

_____

What did you notice about your body as you said, "I am completely calm"?

_____

_____

_____

_____

_____

_____

_____

_____

_____

After doing the activity, can you say that your awareness has increased? Do you think you have better control of your inner world?

_____

_____

_____

_____

_____

_____

_____

GUIDED IMAGERY AND VISUALIZATION

The possibility exists that you saw visualizations when practicing autogenic relaxation. These mental representations bridge the gap between your head and your body, anchoring your thoughts, feelings, and experiences in the here and now. If you're sensitive enough, your senses will almost always give you an accurate reading of the world, whereas your brain can imagine anxiety-provoking events that have little to do with reality. We can recover control of our racing minds by using visualization techniques. Involve as many senses as possible. Using your five senses, conjure up a relaxing "place."

When we overthink, we construct a tense imaginary world in our heads and then drag ourselves into that world as a result. Visualization can be used by oneself with the assistance of a professional or with spoken cues (called "guided imagery"). As with massages, autogenic treatments, and yoga, visualization can all be used together.

It is possible to control our own stress response and relax if we can picture a pleasant scenario in our minds. Don't believe me? Let's try it!

In this portion of the workbook, you will be guided on how to visualize. As a recap, here are the steps to help you with the process:

1. Find a comfortable position and relax your breathing; center yourself and close your eyes.

2. In as much detail as you can, take your time to imagine a location of your choosing, so long as it makes you feel happy, calm, or energized. You might choose a cool, mystical forest, a beach, a snug blanket beside a fire in a library, or even a beautiful crystal palace on a faraway purple planet (it's your image—you do what you like!).

3. As you imagine the details of this place—the way it smells, the colors, the sounds, even how it feels and tastes—also summon up how you want to feel.

Perhaps calm and blissed out, perhaps happy and content. Imagine yourself in the place and see yourself smiling or sitting calmly somewhere.

4. You might create a little story for yourself—maybe you bathe in a glittering fountain that washes away stress, or you talk to a friendly angel, or you picture yourself gathering up an armful of beautiful flowers. Take your time here and spend at least five or ten minutes in this place.

5. Once you feel ready, gently come out of your image, open your eyes, and stretch a little. You might like to include a closing element in the image itself. For example, you can imagine folding up the scene as though it were a painting and putting it in your pocket to access later. Tell yourself that you can always come back here whenever you like.

After doing your own visualization exercise, let's see how you did:

How can you describe your visualizing process? Were you able to imagine a location of your choosing immediately?

_____

_____

_____

_____

_____

_____

_____

_____

Describe the location that you imagined. What kind of place did you visualize?

_____

_____

_____

_____

_____

_____

_____

_____

_____

Can you share the details of your pleasant place? What did it smell like? What colors

can you see? How did you feel when you
were in the place?

_____

_____

_____

_____

_____

_____

_____

_____

_____

_____

What kind of activities did you do in your
pleasant place?

_____

_____

_____

_____

_____

_____

_____

_____

_____

As you were thinking of a pleasant place,
what kind of emotions and thoughts were

you having? Were they positive or
negative?

_____

_____

_____

_____

_____

_____

_____

_____

How did you close the visualization
process? What did you imagine before
opening   your   eyes?

_____

_____

_____

_____

_____

_____

_____

_____

_____

_____

How did you feel after the visualization activity? Did you notice some changes in your stress level?

_____

_____

_____

_____

_____

_____

_____

_____

_____

_____

PROGRESSIVE RELAXATION MUSCLE

Another technique that can help us relax is progressive muscle relaxation. Basically, it is purposely loosening and relaxing your muscles to increase your awareness and control over them. Doctors have long noted that tightening a muscle and then releasing it relaxes it more than before. You can attain deeper muscle relaxation by tensing first, rather than relaxing a stressed muscle.

In the 1930s, Edmund Jacobson stated that if you're physically relaxed, you'll also be psychologically calm. He suggested ten to twenty minutes of daily muscular relaxation. This practice can be introduced to a meditation routine, at the end or beginning of exercise, or as part of your bedtime routine, perhaps accompanied with visualization, journaling, calm reading, prayer, or music.

Now, it's time to practice this technique. It's pretty simple:

1. While in a comfortable position, preferably with eyes closed, move your focus from one body part to the next, first tensing the muscle as tightly as possible, then releasing that tension completely before moving on to the next body part.
2. Begin with the furthest extremities, like fingers and toes, then move inward so you finish with your abdomen and chest, then finally the small muscles of your face and the surface of your scalp. You can also start with your head and

work your way downward if that suits you better.

3. Inhale and contract the muscle as hard as you can for a count of five or ten; exhale fully as you let go completely and suddenly. Notice any differences in the sensations in the muscle (a little guided imagery can help—imagine squeezing tension out of your muscles like a sponge).

4. Finish with a few deep breaths and a stretch; notice how you feel. This technique not only helps you relax physically, but also improves your body awareness, teaching you to pay closer attention to where stress is accumulating in your body. You may even find with time that your intuition about your overall health is improved as you "read" your body more closely.

NOTE: Different body parts must be tensed. Biceps, upper arms, hands, and thighs can be clenched, but shoulders must be shrugged. You should frown deeply and close your eyes firmly. Next, smile widely to strain your jaw and face muscles. If you tighten your stomach, your back will arch dramatically. This may seem like a lot to remember, but after a few tries, you'll instinctively tense the muscles.

Once you're done with the exercise, let's proceed to these questions:

How did you find the progressive muscle relaxation overall? Were you able to tense your muscles properly?

_____

_____

_____

_____

_____

_____

_____

_____

_____

_____

_____

_____

_____

_____

How did you begin tensing your muscles? Did you start from your head down to your toes? Or from your toes up to your head?

_____

_____

_____

_____

_____

_____

_____

_____

As you were doing the exercise, did you feel any differences in the sensations of your muscles?

_____

_____

_____

_____

_____

_____

_____

_____

_____

_____

Is there a certain area of your body where stress has accumulated? If yes, did you notice any changes in this area after the activity?

_____

_____

_____

_____

_____

_____

_____

After the activity, were there changes in your muscles and mood? Was the activity helpful in relaxing you?

_____

_____

_____

_____

_____

_____

_____

_____

WORRY POSTPONEMENT

Finally, the last technique is worry postponement. It can stop the tension and worry spiral. Worry postponement is a terrific stress-management method for everybody, not just anxiety sufferers.

Worry postponement doesn't eliminate worries (yes, we all have them, even non-anxious people). It means you'll handle worries eventually. Instead of acting on every nervous thought, you wait. You direct your conscious consciousness. Nothing distracts or deters you.

Worry postponement is delaying worrying until later. This is about getting control of your worry and regulating its impact on your life. Worry can appear urgent and all-important, and it can seem mandatory to focus on those ideas and sensations. You can choose.

Setting limits is the key to worry postponement. One strategy is to set a time period to just worry and nothing else. Alternatively, you can limit the amount of time you're worried.

Now, let's do a worry postponement exercise:

First, let's set a date with worrying. Choose a date and time that you can commit to. Make a declaration below:

My worry time is scheduled at _____ a.m./p.m. It will take about __ seconds/minutes/hours.

During your worry time, make sure to use a timer and set it to your desired time limit. While your timer is running, release your worries here. Write everything that comes to mind:

_____

_____

_____

_____

_____

_____

_____

_____

_____

_____

_____

_____

_____

_____

_____

_____

Once the timer's up, re-read what you wrote above. Reflect. Is your worry a genuine problem that needs to be solved right now? Or is it something you can just shove off and not take seriously? Is it even something you can actually ignore?

_____

_____

_____

_____

_____

_____

_____

_____

_____

What is the worry about? What does it focus on? Why do you think this is the cause behind this worrying?

_____

_____

_____

_____

_____

_____

_____

If a friend of yours was having the same worry, what would you tell them?

_____

_____

_____

_____

_____

_____

_____

_____

_____

_____

_____

After this exercise, are you considering having a consistent worry schedule? Why or why not?

_____

_____

_____

_____

_____

_____

_____

_____

_____

What did you think of the exercise overall? Does delaying your worry help in managing your stress? Did it allow you to be more present?

_____

_____

_____

_____

_____

_____

_____

_____

Do you have a favorite among the four relaxation techniques (autogenic training, guided imagery and visualization, progressive muscle relaxation, and worry postponement)? What was the difference in effectiveness for you? Which of them would you most likely include in your routine? Which would you recommend to a friend?

_____

_____

_____

_____

_____

_____

_____

Among the techniques, which do you think are the least beneficial to you? Why?

_____

_____

_____

_____

_____

_____

CHAPTER SUMMARY AND TAKEAWAYS

- You may feel that your anxiety is about to spiral out of control at times. In such instances, you can use proven strategies to relieve stress. First, autogenic training involves sitting or lying down comfortably. While breathing slowly and steadily, tell yourself, "I'm completely calm." Feel your body as you repeat the words.

- Second, guided imagery. Find a comfortable position and think about a place that stimulates your senses (smell, sound, etc.). Any relaxing area will do. Imagine it as vividly as you can.

- Third, progressive muscle relaxation. According to this practice, physical relaxation leads to mental relaxation. So, tense your muscles to relax them. Sit comfortably and strain your body from head to toe or vice versa before relaxing.

- Finally, worry postponement directly interrupts anxiety spirals. When you are worried, schedule a time to worry.

CHAPTER 5: REWIRE YOUR THOUGHT PATTERNS

When it comes to dealing with overthinking, we've built the groundwork in earlier chapters. Taking control of our mental models and attitudes—i.e., including more relaxation into our daily routines and being more proactive with how we use our time—are all guaranteed strategies to reduce worried overthinking and anxiety. Up next, we are going to examine our own thinking.

Mind, body, and emotions influence each other. When it comes to anxiety, the mind is key. Our thinking, mental structures, and cognitive interpretation of the world impact our experience of it. Through cognitive behavioral therapy (CBT), we will seek to go to the basis of our mind's perspective of the world to develop more useful, adaptive thinking.

CBT is generally used to treat anxiety disorders, including panic disorder, OCD, and generalized anxiety, but we may use some of the same tactics to manage everyday stress. Our thoughts (not the outside world) determine how we see and behave in the world. Emotions impact our perceptions, thoughts, and actions. Everything follows our thinking.

In this chapter of the workbook, we'll have exercises to help you identify unhelpful thoughts, confront them, and replace them with more accurate ones. We will work on addressing and working through your anxieties rather than letting them rule you. Instead of anxiously overthinking in circles, use your analytical, mindful, and focused abilities to enhance your life. Before we dive into those exercises, here are some questions for you:

How can you describe your own thinking? Do you think that it contributes to how you process stress? Why or why not? Is there a particular bias toward negativity in your thinking?

_____

_____

_____

_____

_____

_____

_____

_____

What do you usually do when you have unhelpful thoughts? Do you confront them or ignore them?

_____

_____

_____

_____

_____

_____

_____

_____

_____

Do you have overwhelming negative versus positive thoughts? Is there a pattern to what they sound like?

_____

_____

_____

_____

_____

_____

_____

Are you satisfied with your current way of addressing unhelpful thoughts? Or is there anything that you would like to change about it?

_____

_____

_____

_____

_____

_____

_____

_____

_____

UNRAVELING COGNITIVE DISTORTIONS

Let's start by recognizing cognitive distortions, or detrimental attitudes and beliefs. We all view the world via our own expectations, beliefs, values, attitudes, biases, assumptions, or illusions.

Overthinkers tend to believe themselves. We treat our judgments, assumptions, and expectations as facts, ignoring the phase when we added our own interpretation.

As a recap, here are some common cognitive distortions listed in the book. Per distortion, think of a scenario in your life when you may have used such distortion:

All-or-nothing thinking. This is black-and-white thinking. No gray area between right and wrong. You'll know this emotional state from absolute terminology like never, always, absolutely, fully, or nothing. (Ex. When your brain tells you, "Get this right or everything will be ruined forever.)

Is there a scenario in your life that you think you may have used **all-or-nothing thinking**? If yes, give an example below:

_____

_____

_____

_____

_____

_____

_____

_____

_____

_____

_____

_____

_____

Overgeneralization. This is connected to all-or-nothing thinking, when we make broad, all-encompassing generalizations utilizing very little data. (Ex. "All men are like this," or, "This happens all the time," when just one man was like that and the item happened once.)

Is there a scenario in your life that you think you may have used **overgeneralization**? If yes, give an example below:

_____

_____

_____

_____

_____

_____

_____

_____

_____

_____

_____

_____

_____

Personalization. This is another misconception typical in people with maladaptive social assessments and anxiety. Personalizing means "taking it personally." We assume we're to blame for conditions beyond our control, or that random events have meaning for who we are. (Ex. We might see a close friend in an awfully bad mood and immediately assume that we are the cause despite any evidence.)

Is there a scenario in your life that you think you may have used **personalization**? If yes, give an example below:

_____

_____

_____

_____

_____

_____

_____

_____

_____

_____

_____

_____

Internalizing or externalizing. When we internalize, we incorrectly feel we cause phenomena. Self-blame, low self-esteem, and self-reprimanding results in overthinking. Externalizing is blaming others for what's ours. It's not my fault she's upset; she shouldn't be so sensitive. Both distortions eliminate agency and cause powerlessness. (Ex. "It's not my fault she's upset by what I said; she shouldn't be so sensitive.")

Is there a scenario in your life that you think you may have used **internalizing or externalizing**? If yes, give an example below:

_____

_____

_____

_____

_____

_____

_____

_____

_____

_____

_____

_____

_____

_____

Favoring the negative, discounting the positive. This bias refers to our underlying beliefs that things will always be awful, thus we can't perceive the good.

Is there a scenario in your life that you think you may have used **favoring the negative, discounting the positive**? If yes, give an example below:

_____

_____

_____

_____

_____

_____

_____

_____

_____

_____

_____

_____

_____

_____

Emotional reasoning. In this cognitive distortion, we presume that if we experience something, it must be true. (Ex. You have a performance review coming up at your job, and you have a sneaking suspicion that it won't be very flattering.)

Is there a scenario in your life that you think you may have used **emotional reasoning**? If yes, give an example below:

_____

_____

_____

_____

_____

_____

_____

_____

_____

_____

_____

In the following exercise, let's see if you can identify the cognitive distortion tied to your unhelpful thought. Answer the questions as honestly as possible:

In the first column, list at least three unhelpful thoughts you've had recently. After that, carefully analyze the three thoughts. In the second column, identify the cognitive distortion that goes with that unhelpful thought.

Unhelpful Thought	Cognitive Distortion
1.	
2.	
3.	

Look at your answers in the second column. What have you observed about your cognitive distortions? Were you able to uncover a pattern?

_____

_____

_____

_____

_____

_____

_____

_____

_____

_____

_____

Which of the cognitive distortions do you turn out to be using often? Why do you think that you cope this way? Where do you think they come from?

_____

_____

_____

_____

_____

_____

Imagine if you didn't use the cognitive distortions. How would you look at your problems? What would your thoughts sound like?

_____

_____

_____

_____

_____

_____

_____

_____

_____

_____

Do you think being aware of your cognitive distortions can help you manage stress? Why or why not?

_____

_____

_____

_____

_____

_____

_____

The Antecedent-Behavior-Consequence Model (ABC)

In the 1970s, Edward Carr and colleagues found that many problem behaviors had few antecedents and consequences. Though they focused on applied behavioral analysis, the model has been used to frame individual behavior change—in our case, overthinking, rumination, and worry. The ABC model can help you uncover cognitive distortions by examining what comes before (antecedent) and after a thought-inspired behavior (consequence).

As what was discussed in the original book:

The **antecedent** is a trigger that cues a behavior. The **behavior** is the act resulting from the trigger and can be helpful or not so helpful. The **consequence** is the outcome, good or bad, of the behavior.

Outlining these three elements reveals their connection. We don't always realize how our thoughts affect our conduct and how this affects our lives. Sometimes we don't realize what's motivating our behavior, but once we do, we may attempt to avoid or change it rather than the conduct itself.

Here are some examples:

	Antecedent	Behavior	Consequence
Event 1	Being at the grocery store around lunchtime	Picking up a box of donuts and scarfing them all down in the car	Feeling physically sick and ashamed
Event 2	Colleague's birthday at the office	Scarfed down a lot of cake	Feeling physically sick and ashamed
Event 3	Feeling low after an argument with kids	Raided the cupboards for cookies, ate half a box	Feeling out of control

Let's try to do a little analysis on the events above. The three events seem to have a common behavior, right? It's **overeating.** But why? What are the triggers? Let's take a look at the antecedent side. The triggers seem to be a mix of environmental cues and an emotional one. It happens when they are in an environment where there is food or when they feel low after a stressful event. Now, let's head over to the consequences of the behavior. What have you noticed? They all seem to be negative, right?

So what does the log say overall? The behavior is not working because it always leads to negative outcomes. As an added benefit, it gives a path forward: reduce the stressors that cause the behavior to occur.

Now, it's your turn. Let's use the ABC model to examine your own behavior. To do this, first, we have to gather some data. Track yourself for the next three days and fill the table with the antecedents, behaviors, and consequences that you have observed:

	Antecedent	Behavior	Consequence
Day 1			
Day 2			
Day 3			

Once you're done with the data gathering, let's behave like a scientist and look for patterns:

What have you observed in your antecedents? Is there a common denominator?

_____
_____
_____
_____
_____
_____
_____

When you are exposed to the antecedents, what kinds of emotions and thoughts do you begin to have?

_____
_____
_____
_____
_____
_____
_____
_____

What have you observed in your
behaviors? Were they helpful or harmful?
Is there a pattern?

_____

_____

_____

_____

_____

_____

_____

_____

_____

Why do you think that you engaged in such
behaviors? How do you think they were
affected by the antecedent?

_____

_____

_____

_____

_____

_____

_____

What have you observed in the consequences? Are they positive or negative?

_____

_____

_____

_____

_____

_____

_____

_____

_____

_____

What are you currently doing to manage these consequences? Are they effective?

_____

_____

_____

_____

_____

_____

_____

_____

_____

_____

Is there anything you would like to change on how you respond to your antecedents? Are there behaviors that you want to replace? Do you want to have desirable consequences?

_____

_____

_____

_____

_____

_____

_____

_____

_____

_____

_____

_____

_____

_____

_____

_____

_____

_____

_____

Look at your entries per day and let's try to uncover your thoughts behind those behaviors.

	Thought *(Ex. If I eat cookies, I will feel better after having an argument with my children.)*
Day 1	
Day 2	
Day 3	

What have you observed with the thoughts you have? Were they helpful or unhelpful? If they are unhelpful, can you recognize the cognitive distortion tied to the thought?

_____

_____

_____

_____

_____

_____

_____

_____

_____

_____

What is the theme of your unhelpful thoughts? What do they usually center on?

_____

_____

_____

_____

_____

_____

_____

_____

What do you think are the sources of these unhelpful thoughts? What do they have in common? Did you notice a pattern?

_____

_____

_____

_____

_____

_____

_____

_____

_____

How did you feel using the ABC method? Did you find it effective in examining your behaviors and their triggers? Why or why not?

_____

_____

_____

_____

_____

_____

_____

_____

Keep a Dysfunctional Thought Record

Work directly with maladaptive thoughts, especially those causing unwanted behaviors, to lessen overthinking and worry. A "dysfunctional thought record" is a means to collect automatic, unconscious thoughts so we can study them and decide if an alternative would be preferable.

Creating a thinking record is just like an ABC spreadsheet. A filled-out dysfunctional thought record can look like this:

Date and time	Situation	Automatic Thoughts	Emotions	Alternative Response	Outcome
9 July, 10:45	Feeling rushed in the morning, bumping into boss in hallway and unable to answer his question quickly; he laughed	"Others are constantly watching and evaluating me" "I have to appear perfectly in control and correct at all times" "I'm secretly bad at my job and a failure"	Panic (80%) Shame (10%) Feel like I can never relax, feel like an imposter	Possible distortion: catastrophizing, over inflation, focusing on the negative, mind reading.	Feel a lot more comfortable and at ease when I restructure the thought

In the next exercise, you will be learning how to use a dysfunctional thought record table. But for now, let's review the labels on the table above:

Situation: Record any triggering event or environment that comes before certain thoughts and feelings, much as you did for the "antecedents." This could be a memory, thought, emotion, idea, or little daydream that made you feel a certain way.

Automatic thoughts: Put down the resulting thoughts or images, as well as your degree of belief or investment in them.

Emotions: Tease out the emotion that these automatic thoughts inspire, as well as their intensity as a percentage.

Alternative response: Here, after the initial event has passed, think about the cognitive distortions you might have made, and whether you could have had a different, healthier response.

Outcome: Fill this in after you've identified and reworked the original thoughts and feelings. Re-evaluate how you feel, how much you believe the automatic thoughts, the intensity of your feelings, and how you want to act.

Now, it's your turn to use a dysfunctional thought log. For the whole week, observe yourself and fill out the tables on the next pages:

Date and time	Situation	Automatic Thoughts	Emotions	Alternative Response	Outcome

Date and time	Situation	Automatic Thoughts	Emotions	Alternative Response	Outcome

Date and time	Situation	Automatic Thoughts	Emotions	Alternative Response	Outcome

Date and time	Situation	Automatic Thoughts	Emotions	Alternative Response	Outcome

Once you have this table completed, answer the following questions honestly:

What have you observed about the automatic thoughts you have? Do you notice a pattern? How much do you think you believed in them?

_____

_____

_____

_____

_____

_____

How about your emotions? What have you observed about your feelings behind your automatic thoughts? Were they mostly positive or negative?

_____

_____

_____

_____

_____

_____

_____

_____

Let's take a look at your alternative responses. Do they have something in common? What cognitive distortions have you mostly made?

_____

_____

_____

_____

_____

_____

_____

_____

For the outcomes, what changes happened to your emotions and thoughts after identifying them?

_____

_____

_____

_____

_____

_____

_____

_____

_____

How did you feel about the dysfunctional thought log overall? Was it helpful in helping you uncover patterns behind your thoughts and emotions? Why or why not?

_____

_____

_____

_____

_____

_____

_____

_____

_____

_____

_____

GETTING RID OF COGNITIVE DISTORTIONS

Previous activities taught us how to identify and challenge our unhelpful thoughts and triggers. We also learned how to examine our behaviors and their consequences. As we move forward, we will be starting to create the life we want for ourselves. In this section of our workbook, we will learn how to replace these unhelpful thoughts with ones that reflect our values.

Based on the previous exercises about unraveling cognitive distortions, what have you learned about yourself so far?

_____

_____

_____

_____

_____

_____

_____

If you did not have those cognitive distortions, how do you think you would approach life?

_____

_____

_____

_____

_____

_____

_____

Cognitive Restructuring

Albert Ellis is one of the founding fathers of cognitive therapy and cognitive restructuring, where we become aware of and revise unhelpful thought patterns. We can modify limiting or unhelpful thoughts using evidence.

A therapist may encourage someone to collect hard evidence to test their thoughts, assumptions, attributions, and interpretations. Realize that most of what you take for granted has little evidence. And choosing one thought involves choosing another.

Basically, cognitive restructuring is like putting your thoughts on trial. Examining the thought includes gathering evidence against it and for it. Finally, we come to a verdict about the thought. Is the thought accurate overall?

In this exercise, we will be putting a thought to the test. We'll be working with an unhelpful thought and assessing its accuracy:

In the box below, write your thought that you want to be examined:

┌─────────────────────────────────────┐
│   │
│   │
│   │
│   │
│   │
└─────────────────────────────────────┘

What do you think is the source of this thought? Do you think the source is reliable?

_____

_____

_____

_____

_____

_____

_____

_____

_____

_____

_____

_____

Do you have any evidence to prove that this thought is true?

_____

_____

_____

_____

_____

_____

_____

_____

_____

Do you have any evidence to prove that this thought is false?

_____

_____

_____

_____

_____

_____

_____

_____

_____

_____

Weigh the evidence you gathered. Was it mostly supportive or against the thought?

_____

_____

_____

_____

_____

_____

_____

_____

_____

_____

Is the thought a genuine one or something you have because of habit?

_____

_____

_____

_____

_____

_____

_____

_____

_____

Do you think that there's a cognitive distortion behind the thought? If yes, can you identify the cognitive distortion that was used?

_____

_____

_____

_____

_____

_____

_____

_____

_____

_____

What would be your immediate reaction if you found out that a friend or loved one was having the same thought?

_____

_____

_____

_____

_____

_____

_____

_____

Look at the evidence you gathered. Do you think that it is enough for you to arrive at a conclusion? If so, what is your final verdict about the thought?

_____

_____

_____

_____

_____

_____

_____

_____

_____

_____

After doing the activity, did you notice some changes in how you view your initial thought?

_____

_____

_____

_____

_____

_____

_____

_____

How did you feel about the exercise overall? Was it effective in helping you restructure your thoughts?

_____

_____

_____

_____

_____

_____

_____

_____

_____

_____

Behavioral Experiments

While looking for evidence to support our beliefs might be helpful, it is sometimes necessary to conduct our own "experiments" in order to demonstrate that our beliefs are not based in reality. The emotional component of stubborn fundamental beliefs means they won't go away just because you intellectually argue against them. We need to act on them too.

In this section, you will be learning how to conduct a behavioral experiment. As a review, here are the steps to do it:

- Clarify the belief
- Create a hypothesis
- Create an experiment
- Run the experiment
- Analyze the results
- Make adjustments

STEP 1: Clarify the belief

In the box below, write a belief that you want to clarify:

What are the emotions tied to this thought? Can you describe their intensity?

_____

_____

_____

_____

_____

_____

_____

_____

STEP 2: Create a hypothesis

What is the potential alternative of that belief? (Ex. If the thought is, "Everyone hates me," the potential alternative is, "Some people don't hate me.")

_____

_____

_____

_____

_____

_____

_____

_____

STEP 3: Create an experiment

What do you need to do to put your hypothesis to the test? (Ex. I will observe the people around me for a week and see if they display any hateful behavior toward me.)

_____

_____

_____

_____

_____

_____

_____

_____

STEP 4: Run the experiment

After doing the experiment you mentioned in STEP 3, let's gather some data.

In the space below, list your observations from your experiment. What did you notice as you were doing the experiment? (Ex. For a week, I have observed that at least three people reached out to me and asked me to hang out.)

_____

_____

_____

_____

_____

_____

_____

STEP 5: Analyze the results

Based on the results, what conclusion can you make? (Ex. I observed that people did not display any hateful behavior toward me.)

_____

_____

_____

_____

_____

_____

_____

_____

How do you look at your original belief now? How do you feel about it? What did the evidence tell you?

_____

_____

_____

_____

_____

_____

_____

_____

STEP 6: Make adjustments

Are you satisfied with the conclusion you came up with? Why or why not?

_____

_____

_____

_____

_____

_____

_____

_____

_____

If ever the same belief occurs in the future, are you willing to do a behavioral experiment to test it out?

_____

_____

_____

_____

_____

_____

_____

_____

Another method to conduct a behavioral experiment is to utilize surveys. For this exercise, you will look for people who have similar thoughts as you and ask their experience about it.

There are a lot of ways to do this. You can simply do a Google search and personally message the people you can find if they provided details. Another is to post a question on sites like Reddit or Quora. For example, if you have a belief that everybody hates you, you can simply ask the question, "Do you ever feel like everybody hates you? What do you do to challenge this feeling?" People with the same experience will respond and share their thoughts.

With the options above, which would you prefer doing to help you look for people with the same thoughts as you? Do you have another way that you would like to try that wasn't in the options?

_____

_____

_____

_____

_____

Spend a day looking for people and interacting with them, and reflect afterward. What did you learn about the other people who have the same thoughts as you?

_____

_____

_____

_____

_____

_____

How did you feel about the activity overall? Was it helpful in normalizing your own thoughts? How do you view them now?

_____

_____

_____

_____

_____

_____

Third, there are discovery experiments. Anxious people often have false beliefs about others, the world, and themselves. They've internalized their unreasonable concerns so much that they can't consider alternatives.

This experiment is different from hypothesis testing because you're not analyzing a statement or thought. You enact it to watch how others react. For many, this is the only way to find out if what they believe is real, because introspection and thinking things through are ineffective. This experiment will convince you the most because your own experience will speak for itself.

In this exercise, let's use the belief you answered in the previous activity. Write it down below:

Now, act as if you don't have this belief. Observe what happens. List your observations below:

_____

_____

_____

_____

_____

_____

_____

_____

_____

_____

_____

How did you feel about the experience? What conclusions were you able to draw from it?

_____

_____

_____

_____

_____

_____

_____

_____

How did you feel about the discovery experiment overall? Was it effective in helping you assess if what you think is true or not?

_____

_____

_____

_____

_____

_____

_____

_____

_____

USING CBT TO CLEAN UP YOUR SELF-TALK

Cognitive behavioral therapy (CBT) can help us manage chronic low self-esteem, self-judgment, and self-doubt. Using the ABC framework or dysfunctional thought record, we can observe what drives our self-talk, which can be tough because it's often unconscious and ongoing. Use these recordings to find a single emotional theme behind your self-talk and a basic idea or concept that triggers it.

The healthier alternative to chronic, deep-seated self-talk is frequently emotional. Instead of obsessing on the precision, truth, or logic of your thoughts, you may need to understand the emotion underlying it.

Now, take your time to look back on your previous exercises. Observe your entries. What do they say about your self-talk? Do you talk to yourself in a positive or negative light?

_____

_____

_____

What do you think causes you to talk to yourself that way? What are the emotions that come with it?

_____

_____

_____

_____

_____

_____

_____

_____

_____

What do you think is the common theme of your internal dialogue?

_____

_____

_____

_____

_____

_____

_____

_____

_____

_____

_____

How has your internal dialogue impacted
your life? Did it affect your life positively
or negatively?

_____

_____

_____

_____

_____

_____

_____

_____

Are you satisfied with the way you talk to
yourself, or is there something you would
like to change or improve?

_____

_____

_____

_____

_____

_____

_____

_____

SELF-SCRIPTING: FOSTERING AND REINFORCING POSITIVE SELF-TALK

A "self-script" is a constantly positive and encouraging style of talking to and about yourself.

A self-script controls our inner conversation. If you can self-script amid stress and overthinking, it may become habitual. Self-scripts can be used for meditation, visualization, or progressive muscle relaxation, or combined with mantras and uplifting phrases. Create an uplifting self-talk script when you're strong and cheerful, then use it when you're anxious or distressed.

Self-scripts are like self-hypnosis and direct your attention. A self-script allows you to control your unconscious self-talk. Put significant phrases on your wall or write them down. After a while, note mood and thought changes (if any) and make adjustments. Distinct situations, triggers, cognitive distortions, or anxieties can have different scripts.

Now, it's time for you to create a self-script. Remember to focus on making positive and affirming statements. What would you like to tell yourself during stressful times?

TIP: Use I-statements to help you change your thought process.

Practice saying this script a few times. Did you notice any changes in your mood? Describe the changes below:

_____

_____

_____

_____

_____

_____

_____

_____

What is the big change between your script and your normal self-narrative?

_____

_____

_____

_____

_____

_____

_____

_____

_____

How did you feel about creating your self-script? Why do you think you came up with such a script?

_____

_____

_____

_____

_____

_____

_____

Do you think that your self-script can help you calm down in times of distress? Why or why not?

_____

_____

_____

_____

_____

_____

_____

_____

_____

_____

CHAPTER SUMMARY AND TAKEAWAYS

- We're locked in negative thought patterns that give us distress. Cognitive behavioral therapy can help you recognize and replace negative thought patterns with good ones, improving your mental health.

- First, identify your cognitive distortions. Black-and-white thinking, where everything is either dreadful or heavenly, and ignoring the good to focus on the bad are widespread. We presumably use multiple distortions at once.

- Next, we ask what situations, individuals, or settings trigger your thought patterns. Use the dysfunctional thinking record to track details. Whenever you slide into a negative thought pattern, identify the place, setting, or events that preceded it, the idea, and its distortion. Then, consider a sensible reaction.

- Once we recognize cognitive distortions, we must adjust our thinking. Behavioral experiments can help. Simply state your negative thoughts or beliefs. Then develop a hypothesis. Consider whether you have proof or past experience to disprove the notion. If you find grounds to dispute your original belief, study them and adjust your mental habits.

- Lastly, create a self-script that you can use the next time you encounter a stressful event. Remember, the language we use while talking to ourselves is as important as accuracy. Our mental dialogue is more than a single thought; it's an attitude and a habit. Like any other connection, we can create a compassionate and respectful script and mental dialogue with ourselves.

CHAPTER 6: NEWFOUND ATTITUDES AND EMOTIONAL REGULATION

In earlier chapters, we've looked at overthinking (which is anxiety) from many sides and covered methods including managing time and life stresses and controlling your own ideas, emotions, and behavior. By doing the said methods regularly, one can learn how to adopt a calm mindset.

In this chapter, we'll concentrate on developing the attitude of a non-anxious person. As was discussed in the original book, it's a five-attitude "manifesto" towards calm. A calm person may have one or more of the mindsets. But before we explore those attitudes, let's have a little reflection.

What is your current attitude toward the obstacles you face in life? Do you face them calmly or anxiously?

_____

_____

_____

_____

_____

_____

_____

_____

What do you like most about your attitude toward life challenges? What do you like least?

_____

_____

_____

_____

_____

_____

_____

_____

_____

Are you satisfied with your mindset? Or is there something about it that you want to improve or change?

_____

_____

_____

_____

_____

_____

_____

_____

_____

Do you think that your mindset has a huge influence on how you process stress?

_____

_____

_____

_____

_____

_____

_____

_____

_____

_____

_____

ATTITUDE 1: FOCUS ON WHAT YOU CAN CONTROL, NOT ON WHAT YOU CAN'T

When we're weak and helpless, we overthink. When we focus on outside factors, we feel powerless. We ignore all the ways we can make improvements, and obsess on what bothers us without any agency. We fixate on things we can't change and overlook alternative possibilities and responses. We need to focus on the solutions.

It's human to get scared, angry, or sad in stressful situations. But what would a Stoic do? They would accept what they couldn't alter. Epictetus, an ancient Stoic, said, "Just keep in mind: the more we value things outside our control, the less control we have." Outside events have no power over us. If we keep focusing on outside events we can't control, we'll feel powerless and anxious.

Other people's opinions	Past	My attitude
Social media	Sickness	My thoughts
Self-care	My spirituality	Internet connection
My friend's sexual preferences	How I react	Political news
Natural disasters	My parents' expectations	Traffic

Based on the words above, identify the things that you think you can control and those that you can't. Fill in the table on the next page:

Things I cannot control:	Things I can control:

If you're being completely honest with yourself, which of the following do you now devote the majority of your time and attention to?

_____

_____

_____

_____

_____

_____

_____

_____

Is there anything you want to add to the list but was not in the choices? What are those?

_____

_____

_____

_____

_____

_____

_____

_____

What can you do to focus more on the things you can control? What would your situation look like if you put more attention on things you can control?

_____

_____

_____

_____

_____

_____

_____

_____

_____

How does it feel to completely ignore what you cannot control?

_____

_____

_____

_____

_____

_____

_____

_____

_____

Is there any actual purpose to thinking about the things you cannot control?

_____

_____

_____

_____

_____

_____

_____

_____

_____

Do you think that focusing more on what you can control than on what you can't is a good mindset to help you approach life better? Why or why not?

_____

_____

_____

_____

_____

_____

_____

_____

_____

ATTITUDE 2: FOCUS ON WHAT YOU CAN DO, NOT ON WHAT YOU CAN'T

Anxiety and overthinking are abstract, internal, and imprecise. It's all possibilities, anxieties, what-ifs, memories, and conjecture—air. If you live in your thoughts, you may feel disempowered, as if you were simply there to passively observe the world and ponder, rather than being an active participant. Sometimes we overthink because we're afraid to act, feel we can't act, or don't realize we can and should act.

Action can clear up confusion and stress-inducing rumination. If you don't focus on action, or worry about what can't be done, you'll feel frustrated and useless. We stress over impotence and ignore solutions.

Ideally, we can use our cognitive powers to solve issues, conjure up inventive solutions, or find a fresh way through a weird new scenario. Thinking is a priceless skill if it motivates action. Action without thinking is foolishness, while thinking without action is anxiety.

When faced with life's challenges, what is your initial reaction most of the time: confusion or confidence? Why?

_____

_____

_____

_____

_____

_____

_____

_____

Think of a problem you had recently. What actions did you do toward solving the problem? Were you able to perform these actions immediately?

_____

_____

_____

_____

_____

_____

_____

Do you have any struggles in taking action when solving your problems? What do you think is the cause of this?

_____

_____

_____

_____

_____

_____

_____

_____

_____

When you feel like you're stuck on a problem, what do you do to motivate yourself to think of solutions?

_____

_____

_____

_____

_____

_____

_____

_____

_____

How does it feel to take action versus merely think more?

_____

_____

_____

_____

_____

_____

_____

_____

What can you do to focus more on what you can do? If you think you put more energy into taking action, will it solve your problem effectively?

_____

_____

_____

_____

_____

_____

_____

_____

_____

Do you think that focusing more on what you can do than on what you can't is an important mindset? Why or why not?

_____

_____

_____

_____

_____

_____

_____

_____

ATTITUDE 3: FOCUS ON WHAT YOU HAVE, NOT ON WHAT YOU DON'T HAVE

Focusing on what you have will help you view any circumstance positively. It's easier to see solutions and new opportunities with this mindset. When you focus on what's missing, lacking, or bad, that's all you see. If you're not focused, you can overlook the solution to your misery.

Look at your life right now. Can you say that you are fully satisfied with what you have?

_____

_____

_____

_____

_____

_____

_____

_____

Among the things you have right now, which of them are you the most grateful for?

_____

_____

_____

_____

_____

_____

_____

_____

Have you ever felt that there is something missing or lacking in your life? If yes, what is it? How do you feel that you don't have it?

_____

_____

_____

_____

_____

_____

_____

_____

When you have a problem, are you quick to appreciate and maximize your current resources, or do you tend to look for something that you don't have? Why do you think you react this way?

_____

_____

_____

_____

_____

_____

Is there anything you can do to better appreciate what you already have? Do you think that having this mindset can help you better in life?

_____

_____

_____

_____

_____

_____

_____

_____

_____

ATTITUDE 4: FOCUS ON THE PRESENT, NOT THE PAST OR THE FUTURE

Focusing on the present reduces overthinking. Focus your thoughts where they'll be most helpful. Any solution, enjoyment, insight, or beneficial action is here in the present, not in the past or future.

Can you say that you are a "now" person? Or does your mind frequently wander in the past or future? Why do you think so?

_____

_____

_____

_____

_____

_____

_____

_____

When experiencing something new, do you tend to enjoy or worry? Why do you think you react this way?

_____

_____

_____

_____

_____

_____

_____

_____

_____

Do you think your past actions or future worries influence the way you make decisions in the present? Give an example of how it happened in your life.

_____

_____

_____

_____

_____

_____

_____

_____

_____

If someone tells you to live in the present moment, do you find it easy or difficult to do? Why or why not?

_____

_____

_____

_____

_____

_____

_____

_____

_____

If you want to be mindful of the present, what activities do you usually do? Are they effective?

_____

_____

_____

_____

_____

_____

_____

_____

_____

If you focus more on what's here in the present, will there be a difference in how you approach life? Do you think this is a helpful mindset to have? Why or why not?

_____

_____

_____

_____

_____

_____

_____

_____

_____

ATTITUDE 5: FOCUS ON WHAT YOU NEED, NOT WHAT YOU WANT

Inner narratives and self-talk can create complicated universes unrelated to reality. Misunderstanding what's essential to our pleasure and well-being might lead to tense overthinking. Focusing on needs rather than wants helps you prioritize what's important. Focus on what counts and let go of the rest.

How do you distinguish your needs from your wants? Which of them do you spend more time meeting?

_____

_____

_____

_____

_____

_____

_____

_____

_____

_____

_____

Make a list of your top five needs and explain why they matter to you.

NEED *(Ex. I have a need for social support.)*	WHY IT MATTERS TO ME *(My need for social support matters to me because in times of crisis, I need people to help me see things objectively.)*
1.	
2.	
3.	
4.	
5.	

Do you always have these wants met? If so, what do you do to make sure they are always met? If not, what do you think is preventing you from prioritizing them?

_____

_____

_____

_____

_____

_____

_____

_____

_____

Do you always have these needs met? If so, what do you do to make sure they are always met? If not, what do you think is preventing you from prioritizing them?

_____

_____

_____

_____

_____

_____

_____

Which one makes you feel fulfilled or satisfied—getting your wants or getting your needs? Why?

_____

_____

_____

_____

_____

_____

_____

_____

What do you think is the difference between focusing on your needs versus focusing on your wants?

_____

_____

_____

_____

_____

_____

_____

_____

_____

Imagine yourself putting your wants first, then your needs. What do you think your life will look like? Do you like what you see?

_____

_____

_____

_____

_____

_____

_____

Now imagine yourself putting your needs first, then your wants. What do you think your life will look like? Do you think having this mindset can help you in life? Why or why not?

_____

_____

_____

_____

_____

_____

_____

Out of the five attitudes, which do you think are the most beneficial? Why?

_____

_____

_____

_____

_____

_____

_____

_____

Out of the five attitudes, which do you think you already have? Which of them are you considering learning?

_____

_____

_____

_____

_____

_____

_____

_____

_____

_____

EMOTION REGULATION VIA THE OPPOSITE ACTION

The attitudes discussed in the previous exercises shape our thinking, perception, behavior, and world. They are important to have positivity, adaptability, hope, thankfulness, curiosity, patience, self-respect, and good humor. When we know and master our emotions, we may choose the best emotional state. Mastery of self includes body, mind, and heart (emotions).

CBT and mindfulness teach us to sit with our emotions without judgment. We calmly accept what we feel. Emotional regulation starts with acceptance. We learn to manage our emotions by naming them and getting to know them.

One helpful technique is the opposite action strategy. It involves doing the opposite of what your emotions tell you. This doesn't mean denial or fighting real emotion. To use this strategy, we must first consider how we feel when we overthink.

We were able to identify unhealthy thoughts using our CBT spreadsheet, but the opposite action technique allows us to find out the emotional foundation of these thoughts so that we can try out a better option that feels better. In the following exercises, you will learn how to use the opposite action technique.

Think of a stressful situation that you encountered recently. (You can use something you mentioned in the previous chapter or something entirely new.) Give a summary of what you experienced.

_____

_____

_____

_____

_____

_____

_____

_____

_____

_____

_____

_____

What kind of feelings did you have during the situation?

_____

_____

_____

_____

_____

_____

_____

_____

_____

Pay attention to the thoughts and actions that these emotions are influencing you to engage in. Are you happy with the way you're thinking and acting, and are these emotions serving your goals and values? In your opinion, are they a threat to your well-being?

_____

_____

_____

_____

_____

_____

_____

Now, let's bring some balance to your state of mind. What is the opposite of the emotion you felt?

_____

_____

_____

_____

_____

_____

_____

_____

For the following days, try to commit to maintaining the opposite emotion. What can you think of doing to make this happen?

_____

_____

_____

_____

_____

_____

_____

_____

_____

Observe yourself in the following days before answering this question. What were the results? What have you noticed about your thoughts and actions when you committed to feeling the opposite emotion?

_____

_____

_____

_____

_____

_____

_____

_____

_____

How did you feel about the activity overall? Was it useful in regulating your emotions and bringing balance to your state of mind?

_____

_____

_____

_____

_____

A WORD ON RUMINATING

There are many definitions of "ruminating." This word has already been used a few times in this text, but its meaning has never been clearly defined.

The Latin root of the word "ruminare" means "to chew over," which explains the word's etymology. The term "ruminant" refers to animals that "chew the cud," such as cows. It's a good way to characterize a type of thinking that we all partake in from time to time: speculative thinking. When a cow ruminates, it regurgitates and re-chews partially digested food. Every time we indulge in mental rumination, we are essentially rehashing our past thoughts and memories for the sake of it. While chewing a cud is a healthy and natural behavior for cows, it is rare for humans to engage in rumination.

In the following exercises, you'll be learning how to understand your ruminating tendencies, as well as develop awareness and distance.

When you ruminate about something, what is it usually about? Describe the kind of thoughts that your mind has during this event.

_____

_____

_____

_____

_____

_____

_____

_____

_____

What do you think is the trigger of your rumination? Does your rumination dwell on a certain emotion such as regret, resentment, or despair?

_____

_____

_____

_____

_____

_____

_____

_____

How long do your rumination episodes usually take? During the episodes, do you usually do something to stop it? Do you do something to distract yourself?

_____

_____

_____

_____

_____

_____

_____

_____

Evaluate the impact of your rumination. When you ruminate, does it improve the situation or solve the issue?

_____

_____

_____

_____

_____

_____

_____

_____

**Think of your rumination as a person.
What would you like to tell him/her?**

_____

_____

_____

_____

_____

_____

_____

_____

_____

_____

**If you are aware that you are ruminating,
how do you think it would change your
approach to your problems?**

_____

_____

_____

_____

_____

_____

How did you feel about the activity overall? Was it useful in making you understand your ruminating tendencies? Were you able to learn how to create awareness and distance from this event?

_____

_____

_____

_____

_____

_____

_____

_____

_____

_____

_____

_____

_____

_____

_____

_____

CHAPTER SUMMARY AND TAKEAWAYS

- After acquiring coping skills for worry and overthinking, it is necessary to transform our attitudes and beliefs for a more transformative impact. You must adopt five such attitudes:

- First, control what you can, not what you can't. Whenever possible, take control. If not, don't fret. You can't change anything, so accept it and go on. The second is to focus on what you can do. This version is more specific.

- Third, focus on what you have, not what you lack. We often overlook what we have while focusing on what's missing. We can fix this by focusing on our good fortune. Fourth, focus on the present, not the past or future. Live in the present, not the past or future, because what-ifs cause overthinking. Lastly, focus on what you need, not what you desire, because you can't have everything you want. This helps you prioritize.

- Overthinking is rumination. Awareness and psychological distance can help. Label thoughts as thoughts, personify or externalize previous stories, and inquire if you're problem-solving or ruminating.

Now that we have reached the end of this workbook, list five things that you were able to learn about yourself and what you will do to address it.

(Ex. I realized that the main trigger of my overthinking is my fear of failure. I will commit to finding out the cognitive distortion behind this and work on replacing it with a helpful thought.)

1._____

_____

_____

2.

3.

4.

5.

Printed in Great Britain
by Amazon

20110742R00149